Healthy Snacks

TARLA DALAL
India's # 1 Cookery Author

S&C
SANJAY & CO.
MUMBAI

Third Printing : 2006

ISBN : 81-86469-89-3

Price: Rs. 89/-

Published & Distributed by : **Sanjay & Company**

353/A-1, Shah & Nahar Industrial Estate, Dhanraj Mill Compound, Lower Parel (W), Mumbai - 400 013. INDIA.
Tel. : (91-22) 2496 8068 • Fax : (91-22) 2496 5876 • E-mail : sanjay@tarladalal.com

---

UK and USA customers can call us on :

UK : 02080029533 • USA : 213-634-1406

For books, Membership on **tarladalal.com**, Subscription for **Cooking & More** and Recipe queries
Timing : 9.30 a.m. to 7.00 p.m. (IST), from Monday to Saturday
Local call charges applicable

Recipe Research & Production Design	**Nutritionist**	**Photography**	**Design**
Arati Fedane	Nisha Katira	Jignesh Jhaveri	Satyamangal Rege
Pradnya Sundararaj	Sapna Kamdar		
	Food Stylist	**Typesetting**	**Printed by :**
	Shubhangi Dhaimade	Adityas Enterprises	Minal Sales Agencies, Mumbai

DISCLAIMER

While every precaution has been taken in the preparation of this book, the publishers and the author assume no responsibility for errors or omissions. Neither is any liability assumed for damages resulting from the use of information contained herein. And of course, no book is a substitute for a qualified medical advice. So it is wiser to modify your dietary patterns under the supervision of a doctor or a nutritionist.

BULK PURCHASES

Tarla Dalal Cookbooks are ideal gifts. If you are interested in buying more than 500 assorted copies of Tarla Dalal Cookbooks at special prices, please contact us at 91-22-2496 8068 or email : sanjay@tarladalal.com

❧ INTRODUCTION ❧

"Heed your hunger pangs, but forget the guilt. With planning and a bit of preparation, you can have healthy snacks on hand so you're ready when temptation strikes".

We all face snack attacks: after work, when the kids are hungry and we're frazzled from a hectic day, late in the evening while watching TV, or on lazy weekend afternoons. Snacking has become a way of life for both adults and children. Many common snack foods are high in fat, sugar and sodium. If these foods are used for snacks frequently, they can affect our health… and their goes all our efforts to lead a healthy life.

Being concerned about this very fact, I, along with my team of chefs and nutritionists, brought together a horde of **40 healthy snack recipes** that are clubbed under 5 different sections.

The section on **'Quick Snacks'** includes quick and easy-to-make recipes. Under the **'School Time Snacks'** section you will find quick and easy healthy snack ideas for your kids when they get home from school. **'Snacks for Entertaining'** is a section that consists of interesting recipes that are sure to gain all the praises at parties. The section on **'Finger Foods'** is flooded with innovative snack ideas to munch on at any time of the day. **'Fruity Snacks'** is a unique section replete with snacks exclusively made with fruits, for all of you to enjoy good health.

This book offers you a wide variety of healthy snacks that will satisfy your hunger, supply your body with energy and provide important nutrients.

So lets all hear it for - Happy and Healthy Snacking!

✒ CONTENTS ❧

BENEFITS OF SNACKING

You may feel mortified about snacking, but snacks aren't necessarily bad. In fact, mini-meals several times a day can prove to be beneficial in many ways:

- Snacks can give you an energy boost to help fuel your body between meals.

- Growing children with tiny appetites may not be able to fulfill their energy needs with only three meals a day. Snacks can provide what may be missing from their meals.

- Teenagers are well known for their snack attacks and for good reason they also have high energy and nutrient needs to support their growing bodies. Carefully chosen snacks can help fuel their growth.

- Selective snacking can help pregnant women meet their extra nutrition needs. Small, frequent snacks can be especially helpful for women who have morning sickness or who always feel full.

- Older adults who can eat only small portions of food at a time may find it easier to maintain their health by eating snacks to supplement their meals.

CHOOSE YOUR SNACKS WISELY

Snacking can help or hurt a carefully charted diet. The difference depends on what you choose and how much you eat. Whether you like to munch, nibble, or simply quench the mid-afternoon "hunger-pangs", you can make snacking work for you. All it takes is a little planning and good snack ideas to choose from. Just so that you forget your bag of chips and junk foods. We've come up with healthier food choices like Baked Potatoes, page 30, Corn Bhel, page 28, Sprouts Dosa, page 62, etc. especially for you!

8

POINTERS FOR SNACKING

- Include snacks as a part of the day's food plan.
- Plan nutritionally well balanced snacks that contain the basic five food groups such as **Cereals** (whole wheat flour, rice flakes (poha), whole wheat bread etc), **Milk and milk products** (paneer, cheese, curds), **Nuts**, lots of **Fresh Fruits and Vegetables** and also **Fluids** in any form.
- Avoid high sugar, fatty and salty snacks, such as candy, chips and pakoras. Snacking on grain-based snacks, for example, can help maintain energy levels while providing carbohydrates, proteins, vitamins and minerals.
- To avoid gaining weight from snacking, keep your food portions small and try to space your meals and snacks three to four hours apart.
- Prepare snacks that are kid-friendly. When shopping, let children help pick out fruits, vegetables, and cheeses for snacks. They will be more interested in eating these foods if they have been involved in selecting them.
- Offer snacks at regular times, such as mid-morning and mid-afternoon. Do not let children nibble constantly during the day.
- Snacks are a good way to introduce new foods. Include a game or activity to learn about the new food and let the child help fix it.

Note: Use full fat milk and milk products (curds, paneer, butter, cheese) while serving these snack recipes to children.

Keep the above tips in mind and make snacking a wholesome experience!

Quick Snacks

Wholesome Submarines

Rich in
PROTEIN
CALCIUM

A *heavy duty snack that not only fills up the stomach, but helps plug in the nutritional requirements of your loved ones!*

Preparation time: 10 minutes.   Cooking time: 10 minutes.   Makes 4 submarines
Baking time: 20 minutes.   Baking temperature: 200°C (400°F).

4 hot dog rolls (brown bread)
1 cup boiled vegetables (French beans, carrots, green peas, potatoes, cauliflower)
½ cup cooked tender corn kernels
1 green chilli, chopped
1 tsp low fat butter
salt and freshly crushed pepper to taste

For the white sauce
2 tsp plain flour (maida)
1 cup low fat milk

1 tsp low fat butter
salt to taste

For the topping
2 tsp grated cooking cheese

For the white sauce
1. Melt the butter, add the flour and cook on a slow flame, while stirring continuously till it turns golden brown.
2. Add the milk gradually while stirring continuously, so that no lumps form and bring it to a boil.
3. Add salt and mix well. Remove from the fire and keep aside.

How to Proceed
1. Slit each roll horizontally. Butter lightly and grill in a preheated oven for about 5 minutes. Keep aside.
2. Mix the boiled vegetables, corn, white sauce, green chilli, salt and pepper and stuff each roll with a little of the mixture.
3. Sprinkle the grated cheese and grill in a hot oven at 200° C (400° F) for 8 to 10 minutes. Serve hot.

Nutritional values per submarine:

Energy	Protein	Carbohydrates	Fat	Calcium
210 cal	7.4 gm	39.0 gm	2.9 gm	90.1 mg

Hare Chane ki Chaat

Tingle the taste bud like none other with this striking combination of green gram and veggies!

Preparation time: 15 minutes.   Cooking time: 5 minutes.   Serves 4.

2 cups boiled fresh green gram (hara chana)
1 cup finely chopped onions
3 to 4 green chillies, finely chopped
1 cup finely chopped tomatoes
1 tsp chaat masala
1 tbsp lemon juice
2 tbsp chopped coriander
2 pinches of sugar
2 tsp oil
salt to taste

For the garnish
2 tbsp chopped raw mango (optional)

1. Heat the oil in a pan, add the onions.
2. Sauté till the onions turn translucent and add the green chillies, green gram, tomatoes, chaat masala and salt and sauté for a further 2 minutes.
3. Add the lemon juice, coriander and sugar and mix well.
   Serve hot garnished with raw mango.

Nutritional values per serving:

Energy	Protein	Carbohydrates	Fat	Calcium	Vitamin A
145 cal	8.4 gm	20.0 gm	3.4 gm	86.4 mg	860.5 mcg

Moong Dal Khandvi

Rich in **CALCIUM FOLIC ACID**

When the hunger pangs strike, be ready with this innovative and healthy snack!

Preparation time: 5 minutes.   Cooking time: 5 minutes.   Serves 2.

½ cup yellow moong dal (split yellow gram) flour
½ cup low fat curds
1 tsp ginger-green chilli paste
a pinch turmeric (haldi) powder
¼ tsp asafoetida (hing)
salt to taste
oil for greasing

For the tempering
1 tsp mustard (rai) seeds
1 tsp white sesame seeds (til)
¼ tsp asafoetida (hing)
2 tsp oil

For the garnish
2 tbsp chopped coriander

1. Combine the moong dal flour, curds, ginger-green chilli paste, turmeric powder, asafoetida and salt and ¼ cup of water and whisk well.
2. Heat the mixture in a non-stick pan and cook for 3 to 4 minutes, while stirring continuously. The mixture is ready when it leaves the sides of the pan.
3. Spread the mixture evenly on the back of three 200 mm. (8") diameter thalis using a flat katori or a palette knife to form a thin layer. Allow to cool for five minutes.
4. Smear the khandvi evenly with oil.
5. Cut into 50 mm. (2") thick strips. Carefully roll up each strip. Keep aside.
6. For the tempering, heat the oil in a pan and add the mustard seeds.
7. When they crackle, add the sesame seeds and asafoetida and pour over the prepared khandvis.
   Serve garnished with the chopped coriander.

Nutritional values per serving:

Energy	Protein	Carbohydrates	Fat	Calcium	Folic acid
97 cal	5.3 gm	12.7 gm	2.8 gm	48.3 mg	26.6 mcg

Quick Green Peas Snack

Rich in VITAMIN C FIBRE

Tiny powerhouse of nutrition… that is what green peas are. Fix up this scrumptious snack for a quick bite… or two!

Preparation time: 15 minutes.   Cooking time: 5 minutes.   Serves 4.

2 cups boiled green peas
½ tsp black pepper powder
¼ tsp chilli powder
¼ tsp ginger powder (soonth)
¼ tsp sugar
1 tbsp amchur (dry mango) powder
½ tsp roasted cumin seed (jeera) powder
1 tbsp chopped mint
1 tbsp low fat butter
salt to taste

1. Heat the butter in a pan, add the green peas, black pepper powder, chilli powder, ginger powder, sugar and salt and cook for 2 to 3 minutes.

2. Add the amchur powder, cumin seed powder and toss well.
3. Remove from the heat, add mint and mix.
   Serve hot.

Nutritional values per serving:

Energy	Protein	Carbohydrates	Fat	Fibre	Vitamin C
100 cal	6.1 gm	13.4 gm	2.3 gm	3.2 mg	7.4 mg

Makai Upma

Rich in
IRON
FIBRE

Picture on facing page.

Get creative! Corn on the cob is a much-used trick; now try this new way to present corn to your family.

Preparation time: 15 minutes.   Cooking time: 15 minutes.   Serves 4.

1½ cups grated tender corn kernels
½ tsp mustard seeds (rai)
½ tsp cumin seeds (jeera)
a pinch asafoetida (hing)
2 green chillies, chopped
1½ cups low fat milk
1 tsp sugar
juice of ½ lemon
2 tsp oil
salt to taste

For the garnish
2 tbsp chopped coriander

MAKAI UPMA : Recipe above →

1. Heat the oil in a pan; add the mustard seeds, cumin seeds, asafoetida and green chillies and fry till the seeds crackle.
2. Add the corn and cook on a slow flame for about 5 minutes.
3. Add the milk, sugar, salt and 1½ cups of water, cover and simmer till the liquid evaporates and the corn is tender.
4. Add the lemon juice and mix well.
   Garnish with coriander and serve hot.

Handy tip: If the mixture becomes too dry, add about half cup of water and heat again.

Nutritional values per serving:

Energy	Protein	Carbohydrates	Fat	Iron	Fibre
160 cal	5.3 gm	27.0 gm	3.4 gm	1.1 mg	1.9 gm

Green Pea Waffles

Say waffles and one can almost smell the exotic aroma... add to that fact a nutritional angle, and you have a perfect snack!

Preparation time: 5 minutes.   Cooking time: 5 minutes.   Makes 2 waffles.

1 cup boiled green peas
½ cup semolina (rawa)
⅓ cup urad dal (split black lentils) flour
1 tbsp low fat curds
3 tsp finely chopped green chillies
1 tsp crushed cumin seeds (jeera)
1 tbsp finely chopped coriander
¼ tsp asafoetida (hing)
½ tsp fruit salt
1 tsp oil
salt to taste

Other ingredients
oil for greasing

1. Grind the green peas in a blender to a coarse paste.
2. Add the semolina, urad dal flour, curds, green chillies, cumin seeds, coriander, asafoetida, salt, oil and ½ cup of water and mix well to make a smooth batter.
3. Add the fruit salt and mix gently.
4. Pre-heat a waffle iron.
5. Grease it lightly with ½ tsp of oil. Pour half the green pea batter and spread evenly. Cook for 2 minutes, until the waffle is golden brown.
6. Repeat with the remaining batter.
   Serve hot.

Nutritional values per waffle:

Energy	Protein	Carbohydrates	Fat	Iron
300 cal	15.6 gm	54.2 gm	5.7 gm	2.8 mg

Moong Dal and Paneer Chila

Rich in
CALCIUM
ZINC

Give the biscuits a pass this tea-time… and opt for this easy-to-make and extremely healthy snack instead!

Preparation time: 5 minutes.   Cooking time: 5 minutes.   Makes 4 chilas.

½ cup yellow moong dal (split yellow gram) flour
½ tsp ginger-garlic chilli paste
a pinch asafoetida (hing)
¼ tsp sugar
½ tsp fruit salt
salt to taste

To be mixed into a topping
¼ cup low fat paneer (cottage cheese), crumbled
2 tbsp chopped coriander
¼ tsp chaat masala

23

Other ingredients
2 tsp oil for cooking

1. Combine the moong dal flour, ginger-green chilli paste, asafoetida, sugar and salt and add enough water to make a thick batter. Add the fruit salt and mix gently.
2. Heat a non-stick tava (griddle), pour a ladleful of the batter on the tava and spread it evenly to make a thin pancake (approx. 5" diameter). Sprinkle a little topping mixture and cook on both sides over a medium flame, using oil.
3. Repeat for the remaining batter to make 3 more chilas.
   Serve hot.

Nutritional values per chila:

Energy	Protein	Carbohydrates	Fat	Calcium	Zinc
95 cal	4.9 gm	12.5 gm	2.7 gm	28.4 mg	0.5 mg

Khakhra Chaat

Rich in VITAMIN A FIBRE

To ensure that your child gets all nutrients, sometimes it pays to be sneaky! Serve these khakhras with the tangy toppings and make sure of your child's health.

Preparation time: 10 minutes.   Cooking time: 10 minutes.   Serves 4.

12 to 15 khakhras, broken into 4 to 6 pieces each

For the topping
½ cup chopped onion
1 tsp grated garlic
4 large tomatoes, blanched, peeled and pureed
¼ cup cubed low fat paneer (cottage cheese)
¼ cup boiled tender sweet corn kernels
¼ cup boiled green peas
½ cup chopped tomatoes
1 green chilli, chopped
1 tsp sugar

1 tsp chilli powder
¼ tsp dried oregano
1 tbsp oil
salt to taste

For the garnish
2 tbsp chopped coriander

For the topping
1. Heat the oil in a pan, add the onions and garlic and sauté till the onion turns translucent.
2. Add the puréed tomatoes and cook till the oil separates.
3. Add the paneer, sweet corn, green peas, tomato, green chilli, sugar, chilli powder, oregano and salt and sauté for 2 to 3 minutes.
4. Remove from the fire and keep aside.

How to proceed
1. Place the khakhra pieces on a serving plate.
2. Top with the topping and garnish with the chopped coriander. Serve immediately.

Nutritional values per serving:

Energy	Protein	Carbohydrates	Fat	Vitamin A	Fibre
265 cal	9.1 gm	49.2 gm	3.7 gm	551.2 mcg	2.7 gm

Corn Bhel

Healthy, delicious and oh-so-simple to make... the corn bhel will rule the roost as one of the all time favourite snack!

Preparation time: 15 minutes.   Cooking time: 5 minutes.   Serves 4.

1½ cups boiled tender corn kernels
2 medium potatoes, boiled and cut into cubes
1 tsp cumin seeds (jeera)
½ cup chopped onions
1 to 2 green chillies, chopped
a pinch asafoetida (hing)
½ cup chopped tomatoes
juice of ½ lemon
2 tbsp chopped coriander
1 tsp sugar
1 tsp oil
salt to taste

For the garnish
2 tbsp chopped coriander

1. Heat the oil in a non-stick pan, add the cumin seeds and allow them to crackle.
2. Add the onions, green chillies, asafoetida and sauté for 2 to 3 minutes, till the onions are translucent.
3. Add the tomatoes, corn, potatoes, lemon juice, coriander, sugar and salt and mix well.
   Garnish with the coriander and serve immediately.

Nutritional values per serving:

Energy	Protein	Carbohydrates	Fat	Vitamin C	Folic acid
101 cal	2.2 gm	18.7 gm	2.7 gm	15.6 mg	19.9 mcg

School Time Snacks

Baked Potatoes

No more worrying over a child's school time treat! Make them this potato and corn snack and watch their eyes glow.

Preparation time: 10 minutes.   Cooking time: 5 minutes.   Serves 4.
Baking time: 40 minutes.   Baking temperature: 200°C (400°F).

4 large potatoes

For the corn filling
1½ cups cooked tender sweet corn kernels
½ cup finely chopped onions
1 green chilli, finely chopped
¼ cup low fat milk mixed with 2 tsp cornflour
2 tsp low fat butter
salt and pepper to taste

For the topping
2 tbsp grated mozarella cheese

1. Wrap the potatoes in an aluminum foil and bake in a hot oven at 200°C (400°F) till tender (about 30 minutes).
2. Cool slightly, remove the foil and split each baked potato horizontally into two.
3. Scoop the potato halves a little so that a slight depression is formed for the filling. Keep aside.

For the corn filling
1. Heat the butter and fry the onions for ½ minute.
2. Add the green chilli and fry again for a few seconds.
3. Add the corn, milk and corn flour mixture, salt and pepper and cook for 2 minutes, till the sauce thickens. Keep aside.

How to proceed
Fill each potato half with the corn filling top with the grated cheese and bake in a hot oven at 200°C (400°F) for 10 minutes. Serve hot.

Nutritional values per serving:

Energy	Protein	Carbohydrates	Fat	Fibre	Folic acid
151 cal	3.5 gm	27.7 gm	3.3 gm	1.2 gm	22.0 mcg

Chilli Paneer and Baby Corn Wrap

Rich in
PROTEIN
ZINC

A typical example of an on-the-go snack, this recipe is the best way to keep your little ones satiated.

Preparation time: 5 minutes.   Cooking time: 5 minutes.   Makes 4 wraps.

4 whole-wheat chapatis

For the chilli paneer and baby corn filling
½ cup low fat paneer (cottage cheese), cut into 25 mm. (1") cubes
½ cup baby corn, boiled and cut into 25 mm. (1") pieces,
¼ cup chopped spring onion whites
½ tsp chopped celery
2 to 3 green chillies, finely chopped
½ tsp chopped garlic
½ tsp chopped ginger
¼ cup chopped capsicum

32

½ cup finely chopped spring onion greens
2 tsp oil

To be mixed together into a soya sauce mixture
1 tsp soya sauce
1 tsp cornflour
½ tsp sugar
salt and pepper to taste
¼ cup water

For the chilli paneer and baby corn filling
1. Heat the oil in a non stick pan add the spring onion whites and sauté for 2 minutes, till the onions turn translucent.
2. Add the celery, green chillies, garlic and ginger and cook for another minute.
3. Add the capsicum, paneer, baby corn and the soya sauce mixture and cook for 2 more minutes, till the sauce thickens and coats the vegetables and paneer.
4. Add the spring onion greens and mix well. Keep aside

How to proceed

1. Divide the chilli paneer and babycorn filling into 4 equal portions.
2. Spread one portion of the filling in the centre of each chapati and roll up tightly.
3. Repeat for the remaining chapatis and filling to make 3 more rolls.
4. To serve, warm the rolls on a hot tava (griddle) and serve.

Nutritional values per wrap:

Energy	Protein	Carbohydrates	Fat	Zinc
195 cal	6.3 gm	35.8 gm	3.3 gm	1.0 mg

Rich Flap Jacks

Picture on page 37.

Super snack for super kids! Rolled oats are rich in calcium and folic acid and thus make for a healthy snack.

> Preparation time: 10 minutes.   No cooking.   Makes 12 pieces.
> Baking time: 25 minutes.   Baking temperature: 200°C (400°F).

½ cup low fat butter, softened
½ cup brown sugar
1½ cups rolled quick - cooking oats
a pinch salt

1. Mix the low fat butter, sugar and salt and beat well using wooden spoon till it is soft and fluffy.
2. Add the oats and mix well.
3. Grease a shallow 175 mm. (7") square tin and press the mixture evenly into the prepared tin.
4. Bake in a pre-heated oven at 200°C (400°F) for 15 to 20 minutes.
5. Cool slightly in the tin.

6. Mark 4 horizontal and 3 vertical cuts with a sharp knife to get 12 pieces. Leave aside to cool.
7. Loosen round the edges. When firm, break into pieces.

Handy tip: Rolled Quick Cooking Oats are available at provision stores under the brand names Baggerys, Harvest Crunch, Champion etc.

Nutritional values per piece:

Energy	Protein	Carbohydrates	Fat	Folic acid
110 cal	1.9 gm	14.1 gm	4.9 gm	3.3 mcg

RICH FLAPJACK : Recipe on page 35. →

Savoury Idli

Rich in IRON FOLIC ACID

Idlis are a healthy snack on their own… but to make them more interesting for your young ones… try this recipe out!

Preparation time: 10 minutes.   Cooking time: 20 minutes.   Makes 12 idlis.
Fermenting time: 6 to 8 hours.

For the idli batter
1 cup rice semolina (idli rawa)
¼ cup beaten rice (jada poha)
¼ cup split black gram (urad dal)
salt to taste
oil for greasing

For the potato bhaji
3 boiled and peeled potatoes
1 tsp mustard seeds (rai)
5 to 6 curry leaves (kadi patta)
4 green chillies, chopped
¾ cup chopped onions

a pinch turmeric powder (haldi)
juice of 1 lemon
¼ cup chopped coriander
2 tsp oil
salt to taste

For the idli batter
1. Wash and soak the idli rawa and beaten rice in water for at least 2 hours.
2. Wash the urad dal thoroughly and soak it in water for at least 2 hours.
3. Blend the idli rawa and beaten rice in a blender to make a smooth batter.
4. Then grind the urad dal separately to a smooth paste using a little water.
   (*The texture of urad dal is different than that of the idli rawa and the beaten rice. Therefore it is essential to soak and grind it separately, to get a smooth paste*).
5. Mix the two batters and add salt. Cover and keep aside for 6 to 8 hours for fermenting.

For the potato bhaji
1. Lightly mash the potatoes and keep aside.
2. Heat the oil in a pan and add the mustard seeds to it.
3. When they crackle, add the curry leaves, green chillies and onions and stir till the onions turn golden brown.

4. Add the mashed potatoes, turmeric, lemon juice, coriander and salt and mix well.
5. Remove from the heat and keep aside

How to proceed
1. Grease the idli stand and spoon some potato bhaji in each mould.
2. Top with 2 tbsp of the idli batter.
3. Steam for 10 to 12 minutes.
4. Cool slightly and unmould the idlis.
   Serve hot.

Nutritional values per idli:

Energy	Protein	Carbohydrates	Fat	Iron	Folic acid
98 cal	2.2 gm	20.0 gm	1.0 gm	0.7 mg	9.5 mcg

Speckled Bubble Bars

An healthier replacement for chocolate bars, these crunchy bars are as good to taste as they are nutritious!

Preparation time: 5 minutes.   Cooking time: 10 minutes.   Makes 6 bars.

1 cup puffed rice (mamra), toasted
¼ cup grated jaggery (gur)
¼ cup sesame seeds (til), toasted
a pinch cardamom powder (elaichi)
oil for greasing

1. Melt the jaggery in a heavy bottomed pan, on a slow flame until it caramelizes.
2. Remove from the fire and add in the rest of the ingredients. Mix well.
3. Pour this mixture onto a greased marble or stone surface.
4. Using a large greased rolling pin, roll out the mixture to a 150 mm. x 112 mm. (6" x 4½") rectangle and 12 mm. (½") thickness.
5. Cut into 75 mm. x 27 mm. (3" x 1½") bars.
6. Cool and break into individual bars.

Store in an air-tight container.

Handy tip: Please ensure that you do not touch this mixture when it is hot, as hot jaggery can cause burns.

Nutritional values per bar:

Energy	Protein	Carbohydrates	Fat	Calcium	Iron
63 cal	1.1 gm	8.8 gm	2.6 gm	78.0 mg	0.8 gm

Beans and Cheese on Toast

Yummy snack for picky children! This recipe is bound to tickle your child's taste buds.

Preparation time: 5 minutes.   Cooking time: 5 minutes.   Makes 4 toasts.
Baking time: 5 minutes.   Baking temperature: 180°C (350°F).

4 slices brown bread
¼ cup mozzarella cheese, diced
4 lettuce leaves
½ cup butter beans (pavta), soaked overnight and boiled
2 tbsp tomato ketchup
½ tsp red chilli flakes (paprika)
2 tsp low fat butter

1. Peel the beans and keep aside.
2. Melt half the butter in a pan and add the red chilli flakes.
3. Add the beans and tomato ketchup and stir for 2 to 3 minutes. Keep aside.
4. Bake the bread slices in a pre-heated oven at 180°C (350°F) for 2 minutes till each is

43

lightly toasted.
5. Place a lettuce leaf on each slice.
6. Spread a generous portion of the baked beans mixture on it.
7. Top with the diced cheese and serve immediately.

Nutritional values per toast:

Energy	Protein	Carbohydrates	Fat	Vitamin A
159 cal	5.7 gm	27.4 gm	3.2 gm	192.3 mcg

Paneer Tikkis

Kids are the most stubborn of eaters. This snack is an ideal way to get them all the required nourishment.

Preparation time: 10 minutes.   Cooking time: 10 minutes.   Makes 10 tikkis.

2 cups low fat paneer (cottage cheese), mashed
2 tbsp chopped coriander
2 green chillies, finely chopped
2 pinches sugar
2 tbsp corn flour
1 tsp chopped cashew nuts
2 tsp chopped raisins
1 tbsp oil for shallow frying
salt to taste

1. Mix the cashew nuts and raisins. Keep aside.
2. Combine the paneer, coriander, green chillies, sugar, corn flour and salt and mix well.

45

3. Divide the mixture into 10 equal portions and shape each portion into small rounds.
4. Press a little in the centre of each round to make a depression.
5. Fill some cashew nut-raisin mixture in it and close.
6. Mould the mixture to form a tikki and roll them in corn flour.
7. Heat the oil in a nonstick pan and cook the tikkis on either side till golden brown in colour.

   Serve hot.

Nutritional values per tikki:

Energy	Protein	Carbohydrates	Fat	Calcium	Zinc
29 cal	0.9 gm	3.6 gm	1.3 gm	29.8 mg	0.1 mg

Veggie Cream Cheese Canapés

Picture on cover.

An innovative way to make sure your children get their share of paneer, curds and veggies!

Preparation time: 10 minutes.   No cooking.   Makes 10 canapés.

5 brown bread slices, lightly buttered

To be mixed together for the topping
1 tsp finely chopped dill (suva bhaji)
¾ cup grated low fat paneer (cottage cheese)
2 tbsp low fat fresh curds
¼ cup finely chopped cucumber
salt and freshly crushed pepper to taste

For the garnish
sliced olives
few sprigs of dill leaves

47

1. Trim the edges of the bread slices.
2. Spread the topping evenly over the buttered side of the bread slices.
3. Cut each slice into 2 triangles, and serve garnished with the sliced olives and dill sprigs.

Nutritional values per canapé:

Energy	Protein	Carbohydrates	Fat	Vitamin A
36 cal	1.3 gm	6.1 gm	0.7 gm	21.5 mcg

Snacks for Entertaining

Corn and Pesto Mini Pizzas

Rich in
FIBRE
IRON

Small is beautiful and these mini pizzas make a splendid treat anytime.

Preparation time: 10 minutes.   Cooking time: 5 minutes.   Makes 10 mini pizzas.
Baking time: 5 minutes.   Baking temperature: 200°C (400°F).

10 mini whole-wheat pizza bases
oil for greasing

For the corn pesto sauce
½ cup boiled tender corn kernels
2 tsp corn flour mixed with ¼ cup water
½ tsp chopped garlic
1 recipe pesto, see below
salt to taste

To be ground into a pesto
1 tbsp chopped basil leaves
2 walnut halves
½ large cloves garlic, chopped
1 tsp olive oil or any other oil
salt to taste

For baking
¼ cup grated mozzarella cheese

For the corn pesto sauce
Mix together all the ingredients in a pan and cook over a medium flame till the mixture dries out. Keep aside.

How to proceed
1. Place the mini pizza bases on a greased baking tray.
2. Spread a tsp of the corn pesto sauce on each pizza base.
3. Sprinkle a little cheese on top of each pizza.
4. Bake in a pre-heated oven at 200°C (400°F) for 4 to 5 minutes or till the cheese has melted.
   Serve hot.

Nutritional values per pizza:

Energy	Protein	Carbohydrates	Fat	Fibre	Iron
112 cal	3.6 gm	17.6 gm	3.4 gm	0.6 gm	1.4 mg

Phudina Aloo

Picture on page 55.

You think of potatoes and your mouth waters. Here is a snack that will further raise the appreciation for it!

Preparation time: 20 minutes.   Cooking time: 15 minutes.   Serves 4.

2 cups baby potatoes
¼ tsp black salt (sanchal)
2 tsp melted low fat butter
1½ tsp corn flour
salt to taste

For the green chutney
1 cup chopped mint leaves (phudina)
½ cup chopped coriander
½ large onion, sliced
juice of 1 lemon
¼ tsp sugar
2 to 4 green chillies, chopped

52

salt to taste

To serve
¼ cup sliced onions
4 lemon wedges

For the green chutney
1. Combine all the ingredients and grind to a smooth paste in a blender using very little water.
2. Refrigerate and use as required.

How to proceed
1. Boil the potatoes in salted water and peel them.
2. Combine all the ingredients together in a bowl and keep aside for 10 minutes.
3. Heat the butter in a non-stick pan, add the potato mixture and sauté over a medium flame for 4 to 5 minutes till the corn flour is cooked and coats the potatoes.
   Serve hot with sliced onions and lemon wedges.

Nutritional values per serving:

Energy	Protein	Carbohydrates	Fat	Vitamin A	Vitamin C
78 cal	1.7 gm	15.3 gm	1.1 gm	390.1 mcg	17.7 mg

Mexican Bean Faheeta

Rich in
CALCIUM
IRON

Throwing a party? Try out this Mexican delicacy… Tortilla stuffed with protein rich bean filling and iron rich green salsa!

Preparation time: 30 minutes.   Cooking time: 10 minutes.   Makes 6 pieces.

6 corn tortillas
4 tbsp grated mozarella cheese

For the refried beans filling
¼ cup kidney beans (rajma), soaked overnight
2 large cloves garlic, finely chopped
1 cup finely chopped onions
1 cup chopped tomatoes
¼ cup finely chopped capsicum
1 tsp chilli powder
1 tsp roasted cumin (jeera) powder
1 tsp oil
salt to taste

PHUDINA ALOO : Recipe on page 52. →

For the green salsa

3 large green tomatoes
½ cup finely chopped onions
2 to 3 green chillies, chopped
2 tsp white vinegar
salt to taste

For the refried beans filling

1. Combine the kidney beans with a little salt and 1½ cups of water and pressure cook till the beans are slightly overcooked.
2. Drain the beans and grind to a coarse paste in a blender. Keep aside.
3. Heat the oil in a non-stick pan, add the garlic and onions and sauté till the onion turns translucent.
4. Add the tomatoes and sauté for another 3 to 4 minutes.
5. Add the ground beans, capsicum, chilli powder, cumin powder and salt mix well.
6. Cook for 5 minutes. Add water if required to adjust the consistency. Keep aside.

For the green salsa

1. Cut the tomatoes into big pieces. Add the onions, green chillies and ¼ cup water and cook.
2. When cooked, blend in a liquidiser and strain.

3. Add the vinegar and salt. Keep aside.

How to proceed
1. Spread a little green salsa on each tortilla.
2. Place some bean filling, fold from both the sides and top with cheese.
3. Grill for a few minutes until the cheese melts.
   Serve hot.

Nutritional values per piece:

Energy	Protein	Carbohydrates	Fat	Calcium	Iron
112 cal	4.9 gm	15.2 gm	3.5 gm	92.5 mg	1.8 mg

Green Peas Pancakes

This ideal snack which boasts of a high folic acid and fibre content is a non-traditional way of making the famous South Indian uttapa. Try it...

Preparation time: 10 minutes. Cooking time: 10 minutes. Makes 15 pancakes.

½ cup rice flour (chawal ka atta)
1 cup boiled green peas
¼ cup Bengal gram flour (besan)
3 green chillies, chopped
¼ tsp turmeric powder (haldi)
salt to taste
2 tsp oil for cooking

To be mixed into a topping
½ cup grated carrots
¼ cup chopped tomatoes
¼ cup grated low fat paneer (cottage cheese)
salt to taste

1. Grind the green peas in a blender to a smooth paste, using very little water.
2. Add the rice flour, Bengal gram flour, green chillies, turmeric powder and salt and mix lightly. Add a little water, if required to adjust the consistency.
3. Spread a little batter round 50 mm. (2") in diameter on a tava.
4. Sprinkle a little topping and smear a little oil on it.
5. When cooked on one side, turn it over and cook the other side for a few seconds.
6. Repeat for the remaining batter and topping.
   Serve hot.

Nutritional values per pancake:

Energy	Protein	Carbohydrates	Fat	Folic acid	Fibre
38 cal	1.4 gm	6.2 gm	0.8 gm	5.2 mcg	0.5 gm

Paneer Wraps

Want to become Ms. Popular? Try serving your guests this paneer-cauliflower stuffed wraps to win their votes!

Preparation time: 25 minutes.   Cooking time: 20 minutes.   Makes 4 wraps.

For the wraps
1½ cups wheat flour (gehun ka atta)
1 tsp oil
½ tsp salt

For the stuffing
1 cup grated cauliflower
1 cup grated low fat paneer (cottage cheese)
3 green chillies, chopped
2 tbsp chopped coriander
2 tsp oil
salt to taste

For the wraps
1. Mix the flour, oil and salt and make smooth and pliable dough by adding enough warm water.
2. Knead the dough well and keep for ½ an hour. Knead again.
3. Divide into 4 portions and roll out each portion into 150 mm. (6") diameter rounds with the help of a little flour.
4. Cook lightly on both sides on a tava (griddle) using a little oil till they are well cooked.

For the stuffing
1. Heat the oil in a kadhai and add the green chillies and cauliflower.
2. Stir-fry till the cauliflower is cooked.
3. Add the paneer, coriander and salt and cook for some time.
4. Divide into 4 equal portions and keep aside.

How to proceed
1. Place a hot wrap on a plate; place a portion of the stuffing on it.
2. Roll it up and serve hot
3. Repeat with the remaining ingredients to make 3 more wraps.

Nutritional values per wrap:

Energy	Protein	Carbohydrates	Fat	Iron
126 cal	4.2 gm	20.4 gm	3.0 gm	1.5 mg

Sprouts Dosa

Rich in
PROTEIN
ZINC

Dosas rock your world... and this super traditional, super nutritious recipe is sure to make your taste buds go into a tizzy!

Preparation time: 10 minutes.   Cooking time: 20 minutes.   Makes 4 dosas.
Soaking time: 2 hours.   Fermenting time: 4 hours.

For the dosa batter
½ cup raw rice
3 tbsp split black gram (urad dal)
2 tbsp cooked rice
5 to 7 fenugreek seeds (methi)
salt to taste

For the stuffing
½ cup boiled mixed sprouts
2 tbsp grated carrot
2 tbsp grated beetroot
2 tbsp grated cabbage
2 tbsp chopped onion

¼ cup finely chopped tomatoes
1 tbsp chopped coriander
¼ tsp mustard seeds (rai)
2 curry leaves (kadi patta)
a pinch turmeric powder (haldi)
a pinch asafoetida (hing)
1 tsp oil
salt to taste

Other ingredients
1 tsp oil for cooking

For the dosa batter
1. Wash the raw rice, urad dal and fenugreek seeds. Soak in a little water along with the cooked rice for at least 2 hours.
2. Grind to a smooth paste with a little water. Cover and keep aside for at least 4 hours. Add salt and mix well.

For the stuffing
1. Heat the oil in a pan, add the mustard seeds, curry leaves and turmeric powder.
2. When the mustard seeds crackle, add the asafoetida. Add the sprouts and all the

63

vegetables to the tempering and mix well.
3. Divide the filling mixture into 4 equal portions and keep aside.

How to proceed
1. Heat and grease a non-stick tava (griddle) with a little oil
2. Pour a ladleful of the batter on the tava and spread it evenly using a circular motion.
3. Drizzle a little oil on the sides to allow cooking.
4. Top with one portion of the filling mixture and spread it evenly over the dosa.
5. When the lower side of the dosa is lightly browned, fold over to make a semi circle.
6. Repeat to make 3 more dosas.
   Serve hot.

Nutritional values per dosa:

Energy	Protein	Carbohydrates	Fat	Zinc
190 cal	6.1 gm	37.4 gm	1.8 gm	0.9 mg

BAKED PALAK METHI PURIS : Recipe on page 68. →

Corn and Potato Tikkis

A simple and subtle blend of ingredients shaped into tikkis that goes well as a teatime snack.

Preparation time: 10 minutes.   Cooking time: 15 minutes.   Makes 4 tikkis.

1 cup boiled tender corn kernels
1 cup boiled and grated potatoes
2 tbsp chopped coriander
2 green chillies, finely chopped
¼ tsp garam masala
2 tsp lemon juice
2 to 3 tbsp bread crumbs
salt to taste

Other ingredients
2 tsp oil for cooking

1. Combine all the ingredients in a bowl and mix well.

2. Divide the mixture into 4 equal portions. Shape each portion into even sized round and flatten the rounds to make tikkis.
3. Heat a non-stick pan and cook each tikki over a high flame, using a little oil until both sides are golden brown in colour.
   Serve hot.

Nutritional values per tikki:

Energy	Protein	Carbohydrates	Fat	Vitamin C	Folic acid
78 cal	1.6 gm	13.0 gm	2.7 gm	7.8 mg	10.2 mcg

Finger Foods

Baked Palak Methi Puris

Picture on page 65.

Low fat puris? Absolutely! This non-traditional way of making puris is not only delicious, but it makes them rich in vitamin A and iron.

Preparation time: 10 minutes.   Baking time: 15 minutes.   Makes 12 puris.
Baking temperature: 180°C (360°F).

½ cup chopped spinach (palak)
¼ cup chopped fenugreek (methi) leaves
¼ cup jowar (white millet) flour
¼ cup bajra (black millet) flour
2 tbsp whole-wheat flour (gehun ka atta)
2 tbsp low fat curds
1 tsp ginger-green chilli paste
1 tsp oil
salt to taste

1. Combine the spinach and fenugreek, add salt and allow to rest for 10 minutes till the liquid is released. Use this liquid to bind the puri dough. Add all the other ingredients and knead into soft dough, using a little water if required.
2. Divide the dough into 12 equal portions.
3. Roll out each portion into a thin circle of about 40 mm. (1½") diameter.
4. Prick the rolled out puris with a fork at regular intervals.
5. Bake in a pre-heated oven at 180°C (360°F) for 10 to 12 minutes or till the puris are golden brown.
   Store in an airtight container.

Nutritional values per puri:

Energy	Protein	Carbohydrates	Fat	Vitamin A	Iron
25 cal	0.8 gm	4.1 gm	0.6 gm	179.6 mcg	0.4 mg

Dhokla Simla Mirch

Picture on page 2.

An excellent finger food that will have you coming back for more! This innovative way of serving Khaman dhokla in a capsicum is a veritable treat.

Preparation time: 15 minutes.   Cooking time: 20 minutes.   Serves 4.

4 large capsicums

To be mixed together for the Khaman dhokla batter
½ cup Bengal gram flour (besan)
1 tbsp semolina (rawa)
¼ tsp citric acid (nimbu ke phool)
1½ tsp sugar
½ tsp green chilli-ginger paste
1 tsp fruit salt
salt to taste

For the tempering
½ tsp mustard seeds (rai)
1 tsp sesame seeds (til)

70

a pinch asafoetida (hing)
4 to 6 curry leaves
2 tsp oil

For the garnish
2 tbsp chopped coriander

1. Cut the capsicums into 2 halves vertically. Remove the seeds carefully so as to retain the shape of the halves. Keep aside
2. Mix together all the ingredients for the batter except the fruit salt using enough water to make a thick batter.
3. Add in the fruit salt, sprinkle a little water over the fruit salt and mix well.
4. Pour the khaman dhokla mixture into each capsicum half. Steam for 10 minutes.
5. Allow the capsicums to cool. Cut each capsicum half into 2 pieces.
6. Heat the oil in a pan, add the mustard seeds and when they crackle, add the sesame seeds, asafoetida and curry leaves.
7. Add the capsicum pieces and sauté for 4 to 5 minutes.
   Garnish with the coriander and serve hot.

Nutritional values per serving:

Energy	Protein	Carbohydrates	Fat	Vitamin A	Vitamin C
115 cal	4.4 gm	16.3 gm	3.7 gm	720.5 mcg	100.4 mg

Grilled Hot N Sweet Paneer

Paneer is an all time favourite with everyone… and this recipe is bound to get tongues on fire with its exquisite blend of tastes!

Preparation time: 15 minutes.   Cooking time: 10 minutes.   Serves 2.

1 cup low fat paneer (cottage cheese), cut into 25 mm. (1") cubes
4 spring onions (including greens), finely chopped
2 tbsp honey
1 tbsp chilli sauce
1 tsp lemon juice
¼ tsp lemon rind
3 cloves garlic, grated
1 tbsp chopped coriander
2 tsp oil
salt to taste

1. Combine all the ingredients in a bowl and mix well. Allow marinating for at least 15 minutes.

2. Arrange the paneer cubes neatly onto 4 wooden skewers and grill them over a charcoal or electric barbecue till they are lightly browned on all sides. You can also cook them on a non-stick pan.
Serve hot.

Nutritional values per serving:

Energy	Protein	Carbohydrates	Fat	Calcium	Zinc
153 cal	4.1 gm	25.5 gm	5.2 gm	158.5 mg	2.4 mg

Masala Sandwich

Picture on facing page.

A filling and nutritious snack… and lip smacking tasty to boot! This quick snack has the goodness of vegetables and whole bread.

Preparation time: 15 minutes.   Cooking time: 15 minutes.   Makes 5 sandwiches.

10 slices brown bread, lightly buttered
5 tsp tomato ketchup

For the potato filling
2 boiled potatoes
1 tsp cumin seeds
3 green chillies, chopped
¾ cup boiled and mashed green peas
3 tsp amchur powder
1 tbsp chopped coriander
½ tsp kalonji (onion seeds)
1 tsp oil
salt to taste

MASALA SANDWICH : Recipe above. →

For garnishing
grated carrots
finely chopped lettuce leaves

For the potato filling
1. Cut the potatoes into very small pieces.
2. Heat the oil and fry the cumin seeds until they turn brown.
3. Add the green chillies and fry again for a while.
4. Add the remaining ingredients and mix well. Allow the mixture to cool a little.
5. Divide the mixture into 5 equal portions. Keep aside.

How to proceed
1. Cut each brown bread slice into a round.
2. Apply butter on one side of 5 bread rounds and tomato ketchup on one side of remaining 5 bread rounds.
3. Put the potato filling on the buttered side of each bread round.
4. Sprinkle grated carrots and lettuce on side of another bread round.
5. Cover with the bread rounds (with the tomato ketchup side on the inside) to make the sandwiches
   Serve immediately.

Nutritional values per sandwich:

Energy	Protein	Carbohydrates	Fat	Iron	Fibre
156 cal	5.3 gm	30.9 gm	1.3 gm	0.9 mg	1.1 gm

Mushroom Olive Crostini

A snack that will take you to the gardens of Italy, this mushroom delight is loaded with nutrients.

Preparation time: 5 minutes. Cooking time: 5 minutes. Makes 6 crostinis.
Baking time: 10 minutes. Baking temperature: 180°C (360°F).

3 large whole wheat bread slices

For the topping
½ cup finely chopped mushrooms
1 tbsp finely chopped onions
¼ green chilli, finely chopped
1 tsp corn flour
¼ cup low fat milk
1 tbsp grated mozzarella cheese
¼ tsp French style mustard
2 to 3 black olives, deseeded and chopped
2 tsp low fat butter
salt and pepper to taste

For the topping
1. Dissolve the cornflour in the milk and keep aside.
2. Heat the butter in a pan; add the onions and green chilli and sauté till the onions are translucent.
3. Add the mushrooms and sauté for a further 2 minutes.
4. Add the corn flour and milk mixture and bring to a boil.
5. Add the cheese, mustard, black olives, salt and pepper and mix well. Cook till the mixture thickens. Keep aside to cool.

How to Proceed
1. Cut the bread into 50 mm. (2") diameter circles, using a cookie cutter. You will get about 6 circles.
2. Lightly butter each bread circle on one side.
3. Arrange the buttered bread circles on a baking tray and bake in a pre-heated oven at 180°C (360°F) for 2 to 3 minutes.
4. Spread the topping mixture generously on top of each bread circle. Bake in a pre-heated oven at 180°C (360°F) for 2 to 3 minutes.
   Serve hot.

Nutritional values per crostini:

Energy	Protein	Carbohydrates	Fat	Folic acid	Iron
53 cal	2.0 gm	6.7 gm	2.0 gm	1.4 mcg	0.3 mg

Corn and Spinach Cream Cracker Snack

Rich in
VITAMIN A
FIBRE

Popeye the Sailor could never do without his spinach… neither would you, after you have tasted this cracker snack. It is a sure fire hit at cocktail parties as well!

Preparation time: 10 minutes. Cooking time: 10 minutes. Makes 12 pieces.
Baking time: 5 minutes. Baking temperature: 200°C (400°F).

1 dozen cream cracker biscuits

For the filling
½ cup boiled tender corn kernels
½ cup chopped spinach
¼ cup chopped onions
2 green chillies, finely chopped
juice of ½ lemon
¼ cup low fat milk
1 tsp plain flour (maida)
1 tsp oil

81

salt and pepper to taste

For the topping
2 tbsp grated mozzarella cheese

For the filling
1. Heat the oil, add the onions and cook for 1 minute.
2. Add the spinach, green chillies and cook for 5 minutes, till the spinach is cooked.
3. Add the corn kernels, milk, flour, salt and pepper and cook over medium flame for 2 to 3 minutes, till the mixture thickens.

How to proceed
1. Spread a little filling on each cream cracker. Top with a little cheese.
2. Grill in a hot oven at 200°C (400°F) for a few minutes.
   Serve hot.

Nutritional values per piece:

Energy	Protein	Carbohydrates	Fat	Vitamin A	Fibre
18 cal	0.7 gm	2.1 gm	0.8 gm	167.6 mcg	0.2 gm

Satay Sticks

A classic combination of a variety of ingredients that have been brought together to make a snack in a jiffy.

Preparation time: 10 minutes.   Cooking time: 8 minutes.   Serves 4.

½ cup low fat paneer (cottage cheese), cut into 12 mm. (½") cubes
½ cup baby corn, cut into 25 mm. (1") pieces
½ cup green or red capsicum, cut into 12 mm. (½") cubes
2 tsp oil

To be mixed into a marinade
2 tsp curry powder
2 tsp lemon juice
2 tsp honey
½ tsp salt
1 tsp oil

For the peanut sauce
½ cup roasted and crushed peanuts

2 tsp jaggery (gur)
2 tsp tamarind water
¼ tsp chilli powder
salt to taste

For the peanut sauce
1. Combine all the ingredients in a pan with ½ cup of water. Mix well.
2. Bring the sauce to a boil. Remove and keep aside.

How to proceed
1. In a large bowl, combine the paneer, baby corn, capsicum and the prepared marinade and toss well.
2. Arrange a piece of paneer, capsicum and baby corn on a toothpick. Repeat for the remaining vegetables (to make approximately 15 sticks).
3. Heat the oil on a tava (griddle) and sauté the satay sticks on all sides till the vegetables brown lightly (approximately 4 to 5 minutes).
   Serve hot with the peanut sauce.

Nutritional values per serving:

Energy	Protein	Carbohydrates	Fat	Vitamin C
178 cal	5.6 gm	15.8 gm	10.7 gm	22.6 mg

GUAVA DRINK, ORANGE SMOOTHIE : Recipe on page 91 & 93. →

Stuffed Mushrooms with Spinach

Rich in CALCIUM ZINC

You love spinach. You love mushroom. Now we bring them together to give you a specially planned nutri-bite!

Preparation time: 5 minutes.   Cooking time: 10 minutes.   Makes 10.

10 fresh large mushrooms
1 tsp low fat butter

For the spinach filling
1½ cups chopped spinach
½ cup chopped onions
2 green chillies, chopped
1 cup low fat milk
1 tbsp plain flour (maida)
1 tsp low fat butter
salt to taste

For the topping
2 tbsp grated mozarella cheese

1. Remove the stems from the mushrooms and wash thoroughly.
2. Chop the stalks finely and keep aside.

For the spinach filling
1. Heat the butter and fry the onions for ½ minute. Add the green chillies and fry for a few seconds.
2. Add the chopped spinach and mushroom stalks and sauté for a couple of minutes.
3. Add the plain flour and sauté for some more time.
4. Add the milk and heat till the mixture thickens. Keep aside.

How to proceed
1. Stuff the cavities of the mushroom caps with the stuffing.
2. Put a little butter in a large frying pan, arrange the stuffed mushrooms and cook for 3 to 4 minutes.
3. When required to serve, top each mushroom with the cheese and cook for 3 to 4 minutes. Serve hot.

Nutritional values per piece:

Energy	Protein	Carbohydrates	Fat	Calcium	Zinc
34 cal	1.8 gm	3.0 gm	1.7 gm	57.7 mg	0.1 mg

Fruity Snacks

Fruit Wonder

A colourful treat for your little darlings, this snack is an interesting, fruity option to give your children a healthy head start.

Preparation time: 10 minutes.   Cooking time: 2 to 3 minutes.   Makes 2 glasses.

4 crushed biscuits (Digestive or Marie)
1½ cups mixed fruits, cubed (apples, banana, pineapple, grapes, orange)
2 tbsp set jelly, finely chopped
1 tbsp sliced almonds.

For the custard sauce:
1 cup low fat milk
2 tsp sugar
2 level tsp custard powder
few drops of vanilla essence

For the custard sauce
1. Put milk to boil with sugar.
2. Mix custard powder with 1 tbsp of cold milk.
3. Add this mixture to the boiling milk and stir continuously for half a minute, till it becomes thick.
4. Cool, add vanilla essence and chill.

How to proceed
1. In a tall glass put half the crushed biscuits, top it with half the chopped fruits, and then with half cup of custard.
2. Garnish it with 1 tbsp of chopped jelly and sliced almonds and serve chilled.
3. Repeat with the remaining ingredients to make one more glass.

Nutritional values per glass:

Energy	Protein	Carbohydrates	Fat	Calcium
304 cal	6.7 gm	43.7 gm	10.4 gm	159.7 mg

✎ Pineapple Passion ✎

Rich in VITAMIN A IRON

We have just one word to describe this passion drink... "Awesome". Once you have had this, high calorie temptations can go take a hike!

Preparation time: 15 minutes.   No cooking.   Makes 4 glasses.

4 cups peeled and cubed pineapple
4 cups peeled and cubed papaya
2 tbsp freshly grated coconut
8 to 12 ice-cubes

1. Blend the pineapple pieces, papaya pieces, coconut and ice-cubes in a liquidizer.
2. Pour into 4 tall glasses.
   Serve immediately.

Nutritional values per glass:

Energy	Protein	Carbohydrates	Fat	Vitamin A	Iron
146 cal	1.8 gm	28.7 gm	2.6 gm	962.3 mcg	4.8 gm

Guava Drink

Picture on page 85.

Here is yet another way of eating the luscious guava! Get all the pleasure of downing a lip-smacking drink.

Preparation time: 10 minutes.   Cooking time: 20 minutes.   Makes 6 glasses.

2 large guavas (amrud, peru)
2 tbsp sugar
juice of ½ lemon
1 tbsp ginger juice

1. Wash and cut the guavas into large cubes.
2. Place these in a saucepan along with the sugar and 1½ cups of water.
3. Bring to a boil and simmer till the guavas are tender.
4. Cool completely and purée in a blender.
5. Add the ginger juice and lemon juice and mix well.
6. Fill half a glass with the pulp and top up with chilled water and serve immediately.
7. Repeat to make 5 more glasses.

Handy tip: To make ginger juice, just grate ginger, place it in a muslin cloth and squeeze out the juice.

Nutritional values per glass:

Energy	Protein	Carbohydrates	Fat	Vitamin C	Fibre
32 cal	0.2 gm	7.5 gm	0.1 gm	46.4 mg	1.1 gm

Orange Smoothie

Picture on page 85.

A tangy, tasty snack guaranteed to make it to your favourite list!

Preparation time: 10 minutes.   No cooking.   Makes 4 glasses.

1½ cups freshly squeezed orange juice
1½ cups low fat curds
2 tbsp sugar
10-12 ice-cubes

1. Blend the orange juice, curds, sugar and ice-cubes in a liquidizer.
2. Pour into 4 glasses.
   Serve chilled.

Nutritional values per glass:

Energy	Protein	Carbohydrates	Fat	Vitamin C	Calcium
59 cal	2.0 gm	12.5 gm	0.2 gm	54.5 mg	94.2 mg

✤ Date and Apple Shake ✤

Rich in
IRON
FIBRE

Hungry at 5 P.M.? Then this is the perfect thing for you… a glassful of energy booster that will put you right back into action!

Preparation time: 20 minutes.   Cooking time: 2 minutes.   Makes 4 glasses.

4 cups low fat milk
1 large apple, chopped
10 black dates, deseeded and finely chopped
a few drops vanilla essence
3 to 4 ice-cubes

1. Soak the dates in ½ cup of warm milk and leave aside for at least 20 minutes.
2. Blend all the ingredients in a liquidizer and pour into 4 individual glasses. Serve chilled.

Nutritional values per glass:

Energy	Protein	Carbohydrates	Fat	Iron	Fibre
127 cal	5.4 gm	25.2 gm	0.6 gm	1.0 mg	1.5 gm

Fruit Chaat ❧ *Rich in VITAMIN A IRON*

This is the perfect snack for all the fussy eaters at home! It is colourfully appealing to the eye and a healthy delight to the body.

Preparation time: 10 minutes. No cooking. Serves 4.

For the chaat
1 cup papaya cubes
¾ cup pineapple cubes
1 cup apple cubes
1 banana, cut into cubes
¼ cup grapes
1 cup cucumber, peeled and cut into cubes
10 to 12 cherry tomatoes, cut into halves
½ cup boiled potatoes, cut into cubes
2 green chillies, finely chopped
1 tbsp chopped coriander

For the seasoning
1 tbsp green chutney
1 tbsp khajur imli ki chutney
¼ tsp black salt (sanchal)
½ tsp roasted cumin seed (jeera) powder
½ tsp chaat masala
¼ tsp chilli powder
juice of ½ lemon
a few sprigs mint leaves
salt to taste

1. Combine all the chaat ingredients in a bowl and toss well with the seasoning.
   Serve immediately.

Nutritional values per serving:

Energy	Protein	Carbohydrates	Fat	Vitamin A	Iron
119 cal	1.8 gm	26.8 gm	0.5 gm	570.3 mcg	2.1 mg

Banana Sesame Pancakes

This fruity snack is likely to transport you to exotic heavens!

Preparation time: 7 minutes.   Cooking time: 10 minutes.   Makes 4 pancakes.

1 banana, mashed
4 tbsp whole-wheat flour (gehun ka atta)
3 tbsp grated jaggery (gur) or sugar
a pinch cardamom (elaichi) powder
2 tsp oil for cooking

For the topping
1 tbsp grated fresh coconut
2 tbsp sesame seeds (til), toasted

To serve
1 tbsp honey

1. Combine the banana, flour, jaggery and cardamom in a bowl and mix well.
2. Add approx. ¼ cup of water to get a batter of coating consistency.
3. Heat oil in a small pan pour a spoonful of the batter on it.
4. Spread it with the back of a round laddle to make a 100 mm. (4") diameter thick pancake.
5. Top with the coconut and sesame mixture and cook the pancake on both sides till golden brown in colour using a little oil.
6. Repeat to make 3 more pancakes.
   Serve hot with honey.

Nutritional values per pancake:

Energy	Protein	Carbohydrates	Fat	Calcium	Zinc
139 cal	1.6 gm	23.6 gm	4.3 gm	32.3 mg	0.3 mg

Fruit Brochettes with Orange Cinnamon Sauce

Rich *in*
VITAMIN C
IRON

Picture on page 1.

Healthy chunks of juicy fruits arranged nattily on a skewer, served with orange cinnamon sauce... is a yummy snack you are sure to enjoy!

Preparation time: 15 minutes.   Cooking time: 5 minutes.   Makes 4 skewers.
Baking time: 5 minutes.   Baking temperature: 200°C (400°F).

2 cups fresh fruits (bananas, oranges, strawberries, apple, pineapple), cut into 1" cubes

To be mixed into a marinade
2 tsp lemon juice
2 tsp powdered sugar

For the orange cinnamon sauce
½ cup orange juice
1 tbsp powdered sugar
½ tsp corn flour
a pinch cinnamon powder (dalchini)

a drop of orange-red colour (optional)

For the orange cinnamon sauce
1. Mix together all the ingredients and heat while stirring continuously till the mixture thickens and has a coating consistency.
2. Strain the sauce and keep aside.

How to proceed
1. Place all the fruits in a shallow dish.
2. Pour the marinade over them and leave to marinate for 10 to 15 minutes.
3. Lift the fruits out of the marinade and arrange different fruits onto 4 thin skewers.
4. Place the skewers in an ovenproof baking dish and grill in a preheated oven at 200°C (400°F) for 2 to 3 minutes. Alternatively, cook on a non-stick pan till lightly browned.
5. Pour the sauce over the brochettes and serve immediately.

Nutritional values per skewer:

Energy	Protein	Carbohydrates	Fat	Vitamin C	Iron
69 cal	0.5 gm	16.4 gm	0.2 gm	26.0 mg	0.7 mg

Basic Recipes

Low Fat Milk

Preparation time: 5 minutes.   Cooking time: 7 minutes.   Makes 1 litre (5 cups).

100 grams skim milk powder
1 litre water

1. Mix the skim milk powder in 1½ cups of water and make a smooth paste.
2. Add the remaining water and mix with a whisk. Boil and use as required.

Nutritional values per cup:

Energy	Protein	Carbohydrates	Fat
71 cal	7.6 gm	10.2 gm	0 gm

Low Fat Curds

Preparation time: 5 cups.   No cooking.   Makes 5 cups.

1 litre low fat milk
1 tbsp low fat curds (made the previous day)

1. Warm the milk.

2. Add the curds, mix well and cover.
3. Keep aside until the curds set (approx. 5 to 6 hours).

Nutritional values per cup:

Energy	Protein	Carbohydrates	Fat
62 cal	5.1 gm	9.4 gm	0 gm

Low Fat Paneer

Preparation time: 30 minutes. Cooking time: 10 minutes.   Makes ¾ cup.

2 cups low fat milk
1 cup low fat curds, beaten

1. Put the milk to boil in a broad pan. When it starts boiling, add the low fat curds and mix well.
2. Remove from the heat and stir gently until the milk curdles.
3. Strain and tie the curdled milk in a muslin cloth. Hang for about half an hour to allow the whey to drain out and use as required.

Handy tip: If you want firm paneer, cover the block with a heavy weight to compress the paneer. This way you will be able to cut cubes from the paneer.

Nutritional values ¾ cup:

Energy	Protein	Carbohydrates	Fat
34 cal	3.0 gm	5.4 gm	0.1 gm